MW00768577

My son, Stacy D. Hilliard, has wr
for the family of God. It has bee
man is an island," and rightly so.
the body of Christ. Moses needed Joshua. David needed Jonathan.
Joshua needed Caleb. If we can prayerfully understand it, Jesus needed
His disciples. One cannot reach his full destiny without the help and
assistance of those that the Father puts in his path. Stacy has caught
this truth and emphasized it. Who do you need? Who have you not
properly appreciated? Properly appreciate your mentors and sons by
getting them this book.

— D. CHRIS THOMPSON, VICE-CHAIRMAN AND EXECUTIVE DIRECTOR
OF EVANGELISM USA, IPHC

I have always been intrigued by the oral ministry of Stacy Hilliard in
his preaching and in the one-on-one conversations I have enjoyed with
him. His unique method of processing truth that is firmly based on
Holy Scriptures has captured my attention and interest.

In my relationship with Stacy over more than a decade, I have
encouraged him to put into writing his thoughts and understanding
of the great truths he has discovered in the Bible. This is his second
book and in it, he has opened my understanding to the importance of
relationships and how to discern their meaning in the exciting process
of bringing into focus the divine destiny God has for each one of us.

As you read this book you will hear God speaking to you in marvelous
ways to help you understand how various people have been used of God
to position you where you were supposed to be. There are some people
who were brought into your life for a short period of time, and we need
to let them go. They were transitional for a certain season.

You will learn more about the value of mentors and the divinely
ordered fathers whom God has given to you to develop your character
and give you a firm foundation to weather the many storms of life you
will encounter.

What Stacy Hilliard has to say to you in the pages of this book will be relevant and helpful in your understanding of your divine destiny. Stacy's use of Scripture and characters of the Bible to illustrate the meaning and importance of relationships will point you to the utterly great and awesome God Who continues to speak within and lives above every page of Holy Scriptures.

— Hugh H. Morgan, Editor, Hugh's News

As I look back on my relationships in Christ, I see many mentors and a spiritual father given to me by God to prepare me and guide me into my destiny as a Christian leader.

At Dynamic Church Planting International, we say, "A mentor is someone who has been where you want to go and is willing to take you there." I have had mentors in my life who have guided me into my spiritual destiny, although neither of us would have called it that at the time.

My spiritual father was a church planter and a pastor. He poured his life into mine, often seeing my needs as a young leader and meeting those needs even before I could see them myself. He loved me and nurtured me and forgave me and pushed me. But most of all he loved me.

Stacy Hilliard's Relationships: A Key to Divine Destiny, along with God's guidance will help you discover the spiritual and human relationships that God intends to help guide you into your spiritual purpose.

Put the words in this book into practice. I believe that they will help you properly discern people and their ordained roles in your life as you access your God-ordained destiny.

— Paul Becker, President & Founder of Dynamic Church Planting International

CONTENTS

FOREWORD

For nearly twenty years I have heard ministers talk about the importance of relationships. There have been times when I thought some were using the word as an excuse, an avoidance of keeping previously made commitments. At times, it felt like "relationship" meant a certain freedom from accountability. Sadly, I have known individuals who have distorted the word and used it for their own selfish ends.

However, I'm convinced that most say the word from a deep sense of longing. Most people are by nature inclined to "put the best foot forward" in life; that is, present ourselves in the best possible light. The late William Sloane Coffin, former pastor of the Riverside Church in New York City, once said in a sermon about putting our best foot forward, that it was a shame we did that so often, "when in reality it's the other foot that really needs attention." How like us to hide "the other foot," that part of us that really needs help, that really needs exposure to light, hope, mercy. We hide because we are afraid, like Adam and Eve hiding in Genesis 3.

Rev. Stacy Hilliard has decades of experience with the diverse dimensions of relationships. A former Marine, police officer, pastor, and now denominational leader, he has surveyed the landscape of relationships. His vast encounters have given him insights into the character and nature of what constitutes authentic relationships. His deep knowledge of the Bible, the Word of God, enables him to move across the centuries within the biblical narrative and bring "old and new" into the present.

Divine and human relationships are centered on authentic engagement with the "other." Sometimes the "Other" is God; sometimes the "other" are the people in our lives. We are not designed to live alone. As John Donne wrote in 1624, "No man is an island, entire of itself; every man is a piece of the continent." This famous line was not written in the context of speculative philosophy. No, Donne, an Anglican priest, was convalescing from illness and reflecting on the needs we have in the difficult places of life.

Stacy Hilliard recognizes this reality that every person faces due to sin. He recognizes that so much of life is really like gaining entrance into heaven: it depends on having a redeemed relationship with Jesus Christ. Finding and fulfilling God's plan for our lives depends on the nature of the relationships we have with people who cross our paths.

This is an important book. It's a quick read, but importantly, it's a rich read. This book will help you discern what the Holy Spirit is doing in and through you with the people who are on life's journey with you.

Dr. A.D. Beacham, Jr.
Presiding Bishop
International Pentecostal Holiness Church

PREFACE

"The kingdom of God is administrated relationally"! Those words pierced my heart as I sat with a group of internationally recognized leaders struggling to find answers for why people were failing to walk out their God ordained purpose and calling. That brief moment gave birth to a belief system that has marked my life and every collegial endeavor in the kingdom since that day. Our destiny is forever affected by our connections, both positively and negatively! Big doors swing on little hinges!

Far too often we have placed our focus on theological astuteness, communication skills, business acumen and spiritual gifting as the primary catalyst for an individuals success or lack thereof. And while I would be the last to minimize their importance, I think we've overlooked what may be the most important ingredient – proper life giving relationships.

The Apostle Paul, in his discourse to the Corinthians, awakens us to the realization that we are interdependent – connected - as a *'many membered body',* each having value, function and responsibility. Those connections are so strategic to our destiny that he concludes his remarks with *'He (the Holy Spirit) sets each member in the body as He wills'* (1 Corinthians 12:12–18). God choses our 'connections' knowing where and to whom we are to be joined for our lives to be fruitful and fulfilled.

In the book you are now reading - *Relationships – Your Key to Divine Destiny* – my friend Stacy Hilliard captures the simple truth that relationships have always been and continue to be God's laboratory for shaping a life and for helping us strategically navigate our way into the *'place'* of our greatest potential. For Stacy, this is not just a principle to be taught, it has been a way of life!

As you read, may you begin to discern the connections God has brought into your life *for such a time as this*! Destiny awaits!

Tony Miller
Bishop – The Gate Church

ACKNOWLEDGMENTS

Special thanks to Presiding Bishop A. D. Beacham and Bishop D. Chris Thompson for your input in this book. I honor you!

My heartfelt appreciation and gratitude to Lydia Jones and Dr. Hugh Morgan for your assistance with editing.

INTRODUCTION

This book highlights the significant role that "relationship" plays in the fulfillment of God's will, plan, and purpose, in and through the lives of His people.

It is vital for people of God to understand that while divine destiny is certainly linked to their relationship with God, destiny is also connected to other people. It cannot be argued that it is God who determines and establishes our personal destiny, but it is also true that He will use people as a part of the process associated with the realization of our destiny. In order for anyone to enter into all that God has ordained for us, we must develop a meaningful relationship with God and with other people as well.

Though it is easy for children of God to see the need for the cultivation of a substantive relationship with God, it is also important to understand that entering into divine destiny will require the proper cultivation of relationships with other people. *The path that leads to a person's destiny will include, in addition to developing a personal relationship with God, the development of personal relationships with people.* I believe many of the challenges that oppose and often cause people to lose out—in part, and in some cases, forfeit their destiny altogether—are not understanding *how vital* others are to their destiny.

The fact that God has factored other individuals into His plan for our life cannot be negated and should not be ignored.

For people who are committed to entering into everything God has prepared for them, the accurate assessment of others and the role they play must not be overlooked. I've found some points to be pertinent in this regard. They are what I call the 3 A's: 1. Acknowledgment, 2. Assessment, and 3. Astuteness.

People who take their divine destiny seriously must first "acknowledge" that God has incorporated others into His overall plan for their lives. Secondly, they must have the keenness to "assess" situations and encounters that will serve as indicators to identify those whom God has given to them to assist in their journey to destiny. Finally, they must possess the "astuteness" to recognize the roles that each person in their life is meant to play.

It is critical that we embrace the fact that other people play a major role in our personal destiny. Not to embrace this reality is to risk missing out on parts of, or even worse, the total forfeiture of divine destiny. *Relationship is a key element to the achievement of purpose.* It is the cornerstone of relevancy in our divine destiny, and it can be seen in God Himself. God is Father, Son, and Holy Spirit, and it's the relationship between all three persons that brings about the will and purposes of the God-Head. *Each person in the Trinity has a unique and distinct function—one in which each member plays a different role.*

While the vastness of God's role in creation is certainly beyond my ability to fully articulate, as it relates to His operation in this world and how He interacts with mankind, I have come to understand the function of the "Father" as "God in Creation," the function of the "Son" as "God in Restoration," and the function of the "Holy Spirit" as "God in Regeneration."

The purpose of the illustration in the previous paragraph is not to create theological debate; I have heard other good illustrations that explain the function of the God-Head. My goal, however, is to illustrate that *each* member of the trinity functions differently, and each *member* is dependent upon the others as it relates to the manifestation of the fullness of God's will—a will that is manifested through a relationship containing such intimacy that the members of the God-Head function as one. I've often heard it said, "God is a relational God." While I understand the sentiment and don't have a problem with its use, I think God desires more than to be "relational." God desires "relationship." Though some may view "relational" and "relationship" through the same lens, I believe such a paradoxical view can be misleading.

Being "relational" with a person does not necessarily mean we are in "relationship" with that person."

In my opinion one word distinguishes "relational" and "relationship": *intimacy*. The fullness of God's will is made manifest through and by the intimate relationship that exists in the God-Head. I've heard many words used to explain the existence of God. While I dare not try to explain God, I believe God's existence can be explained in one word: *relationship*.

God exists as Father, Son, and Holy Spirit—an existence that, by its very nature, highlights the importance of relationship. Truthfully, as it relates to the will of God being accomplished, God is *interdependent*—God depends on God. And, as a part of mankind being made in God's image and likeness, *people are dependent upon people*. This is not to imply, in any sense, that anyone should ever allow another person to take the place of God in his or her life as that equates to idolatry. It is, however, important to understand that our destiny is not limited to just developing a relationship with God; fulfilling destiny will also require the ability to discern and a commitment to developing relationships with the people whom God will involve in the process of preparing and propelling His people into divine destiny.

STEWARDSHIP OF PLACE

"And God said, Let Us make man in Our image, after Our likeness: and let them have dominion over the fish of the sea, and over the fowl of the air, and over every creeping thing that creepeth upon the earth." (Genesis 1:26)

This Scripture passage makes two points clear: 1. a collaborative relationship exists among the members of the trinity, and 2. the process of making man involved each one of them. Being Trinitarian, I have found that people who believe as I do also find the collaborative relationship of the trinity in the making of man easy to accept. In addition to the cooperation exhibited amongst the God-Head concerning the making of man ("let us"…), Genesis 1:26 also makes clear that in order for God's plan(s) for man to be realized, there would have to be relationships in which mankind would have to cooperate/collaborate with one another; thus, "let them…" In other words, the dominion that man is to exercise as a part of the image of God that each of us is ordained to project requires relationships with one another. This is a reality that becomes even clearer with God's mandate that man be fruitful and multiply.

> *"And God blessed them, and God said unto them, Be fruitful, and multiply and replenish the earth, and subdue it: and have dominion over the fish of the sea, and over the fowl of the air, and over every living thing that moveth upon the earth."* (Genesis 1:28)

This Scripture passage clarifies that fruitfulness and multiplication are at the center of God's plan for man. Although this was and still is a significant part of God's desired plan, fruitfulness and multiplication were not and will never be something God brings *out* of man. Yes, God made man with the enablement to be fruitful and multiply, and He mandated man to do so. However, the Bible paints a very clear picture that speaks to the fact it is not God who will bring out of us the fruitfulness and multiplication that He has placed within us; the people whom God will bring into our lives will do this.

After the Lord God formed man and placed him in the Garden of Eden, The Lord God declared that it was not good for Adam to be alone and thus, made the woman.

> *"And the* Lord *God said, It is not good that man should be alone; I will make him a help meet for him."* (Genesis 2:18)

> *"And the* Lord *God caused a deep sleep to come upon Adam, and he slept: and He took one of his ribs, and closed up the flesh instead there; And the rib, which the* Lord *God had taken from man, made He a woman and brought her to the man."* (Genesis 2:21–22)

Important to note is that a relationship existed between God and Adam before the woman was formed and brought into Adam's life. I dare say that God and Adam's relationship was more intimate than we can fathom in our present state of existence and understanding. I believe their relationship was of a dimension and depth that is beyond our human comprehension; albeit, something was missing in Adam's life, and that "something" was "someone." Adam's aloneness had to do with design: God made Adam with needs and desires that God Himself did not intend to meet. And this was not true in Adam's case alone. Adam was, in a sense, the prototype for all of humanity, which means God designed each one of us with needs and desires that will only be fulfilled through relationships with other people. What's even more important is that divine destiny will demand these types of relationships. In Genesis 2:18, when the Lord God said it is not good that the man should be alone, He was addressing more than the issue of human companionship in Adam's life. Also rooted in the Lord God's statement was the issue of purpose. God's mandate for Adam to be fruitful and multiply was

> Adam's aloneness had to do with design: God made Adam with needs and desires that God Himself did not intend to meet.

essential to Adam's purpose. However, this was not something Adam could accomplish by himself, nor was it something God would accomplish for him. Adam was formed and fashioned in a way that enabled him to meet the fruitfulness and multiplication mandate in his life, although fulfilling this mandate was not something Adam could do alone. He needed another person, and it was not just to procreate!

While no one can dispute that procreation is a part of God's plan and purpose for humanity, we must acknowledge that when the Lord God committed to make a "help meet" for the man in Genesis 2:18, procreation was only one part of God's consideration. He considered everything associated with Adam's purpose and destiny—purpose and destiny that God determined would require "help" from someone other than Himself. While the Word of God clearly communicates God's commitment to ensure that Adam was provided with everything he needed to fulfill God's plan for his life, the Bible additionally highlights that God's plan also required the Lord God to make someone and to bring that person into Adam's life. This is a dynamic that should not be overlooked.

Just as Adam could not, by his lonesome, "realize" the destiny God ordained for his life, neither can anyone else. This is because the realization of a self-contained destiny simply does not fit God's pattern or His design as it relates to the destiny God has established for anyone's life—without debate.

People who are committed to being, doing, having and experiencing all that God has incorporated into their purpose and destiny must primarily understand and appreciate their need for others whom God will prepare and bring into their lives and secondarily, possess the spiritual awareness to discern these people when they arrive.

As I stated earlier, the Lord God's making of the woman for Adam addressed much more than procreation. Though marriage and offspring were certainly a part of God's plan for Adam, when, in Genesis 2:18, the Lord God said He would make a "help meet" for the man, the statement was very broad in scope. Finis J. Dake, in his commentary on this verse of Scripture in the Dake Annotated Reference Bible, makes the point that "help meet" should be understood as "help suitable" and was based on moral, intellectual, and physical make-up. It's worth noting that Adam was made perfect in every way—in the image and likeness of God—yet, in order for him to fulfill his purpose and destiny, he needed help that "suited him." While God expressed His commitment to providing Adam with the help he needed when the Lord God made the woman and brought her to Adam, it's important to understand that God determined the woman's suitability. Adam had no say in the matter.

People who are committed to being, doing, having and experiencing all that God has incorporated into their purpose and destiny must primarily understand and appreciate their need for others whom God will prepare and bring into their lives

"And the LORD *God caused a deep sleep to fall upon Adam, and he slept; and He took one of his ribs, and closed up the flesh instead thereof and the rib, which the* LORD *God had taken from man, made He a woman and brought her to the man."* (Genesis 2:21–22)

The Lord God put Adam into a deep sleep before removing his rib and making the woman. Adam had no input! Even though the Lord God took and used a rib from Adam to make the woman, God did not confer with Adam about "how" she should be made. While Scripture does not ascribe whether or not Adam was asleep the entire time, the fact the woman was brought to Adam "after" she was made indicates the Lord God did not form the woman in consultation with Adam.

It was God, not Adam, who determined *who* would be suitable for Adam; and the Lord God made the woman with the qualities, traits, and characteristics God determined to be good for Adam, his purpose, and his destiny. I make this point because although "divinely orchestrated relationships" will require "divine relationships" with other people, it's of utmost importance to understand that *"divine relationships" can only exist between people divinely prepared to be involved.* As a part of His own commitment to the fulfillment of the destiny God establishes for each of us, He will make and prepare people who are good and suitable for us. Then He brings them into our lives for the roles they are to play. The fact that it is God who prepares these people cannot be overstated!

> Although "divine destiny" will require "divinely orchestrated relationships" with other people, it's of utmost importance to understand that *"divine relationships" can exist only between people divinely prepared to be involved.*

In addition to the myriad of things mentioned in association with God's will for man in Genesis 1:26, when God said, "Let us make man in our image, after our likeness…" He articulates that the power to make people, according to His will, rests with God alone. In other words, God designs people after and according to His will. To expect or attempt to make anyone something or someone God has not designed or ordained him or her to be, either for us or to us can be frustrating at best—and at worst, dangerous. To misjudge a person positively or negatively, or misdiagnose their purpose in our lives is a recipe for trouble, turmoil, or even tragedy. This is because of an insufficiency of God's grace to sustain a relationship that He did not ordain. God grants everyone the grace needed to fulfill his or her destiny. This is easily grasped with a basic understanding of how the grace of God is applied to and operates in our personal lives. However, what is often not understood nor given adequate consideration is the degree to which God will use others as both expressions and extensions of the grace He provides in accordance with the destiny God has established for our lives.

It will ultimately be our ability to discern individuals and their roles that will determine whether or not we access the grace that God desires to extend to us through them.

Thus, the proper discernment of people and their roles in our lives is something that should be taken seriously. *While God will make, prepare, and providentially introduce to us the people associated with the purpose and destiny He has established for our lives, it will ultimately be our ability to discern these individuals and their roles that will determine whether or not we access the grace that God desires to extend to us through them.*

Though many have rehearsed the adage, "It is better to be in the right place at the right time than to be the smartest person in town," even better is "to be divinely introduced to the right person at the appointed time." That after making Adam the Lord God put him in the Garden of Eden (Genesis 2:18) meant Adam was in the right place "all the time." However, just being in the right place was not enough. Adam needed the right person whom the Lord God produced for him and would introduce to him at the "appointed time." Scripture makes it clear that Adam was formed first, and the woman was later formed and brought into his life.

> *"...for Adam was formed first, then Eve."* (1 Timothy 2:13)

> *"...And the rib, which the LORD God had taken from man, made he a woman, and brought her to the man."* (Genesis 2:22)

While it is not clear how long Adam was in the Garden of Eden before the woman was made, the fact that she was brought to Adam is a clear indication the issue was not with Adam's location. Given God's preciseness as it relates to order, we must understand that from God's perspective, the woman was made and brought into Adam's life at God's "appointed time." This exemplifies a divine order and pattern, which I don't believe should be ignored.

The personal destiny that God has established for every individual's life will require the successful navigation of various times and seasons in which a healthy understanding of divine timing as it relates to people and relationships is of great benefit. In every season of a person's life, God will use environment, events, circumstances, and so much more as a part of the process needed to prepare them for their next season and ultimately, their destiny. This is something that can be seen in the careful reading of Genesis 2:15–20:

> *"...And the LORD God took the man, and put him into the Garden of Eden to dress it and keep it. And the LORD God commanded the man, saying, of every tree of the garden thou mayest freely eat: but of the tree of the Knowledge of Good and Evil, thou shalt not eat of it: for in the day that thou eatest thereof thou shalt surely die. And the LORD God said, it is not good that the man*

should be alone; I will make him a help meet for him. And out of the ground the LORD God formed every beast of the field, and every fowl of the air; and brought them unto Adam to see what he would call them: and whatso- ever Adam called every living creature, that was the name thereof. And Adam gave names to all cattle, and to the fowl of the air, and to every beast of the field; but for Adam there was not found an help meet for him."

In these Scripture passages, we see the role that things like en- vironment, events, circumstances, and situations played in God's plan for Adam's life—and as was the case with Adam, these things continue to have their place and role in our lives. Likewise, as was also the case with Adam, the greatest contributors to the process by which God prepares and propels us into destiny will be people— people who are prepared by God for an "appointed purpose" and sent into our lives at the "appointed time."

Something often missed or overlooked in Scripture is that al- though it was the Lord God who made the woman and brought her to Adam, the Bible does not indicate the Lord God explaining the woman's role and purpose in Adam's life; this was left for Adam to discern.

"...And the rib, which the LORD God had taken from man, made He a woman, and brought her to the man. And Adam said, This is now bone of my bone, and flesh of my flesh: She shall be called Woman, because she was taken out of Man." (Genesis 2:22–23)

Adam's response, in relation to the woman when the Lord God brought her to him, is of great significance as it relates to his keen discernment; it speaks to the fact that he understood the woman's God-ordained role in his life. Adam recognized her make-up— *"bone of my bone and flesh of my flesh"*—as well as her purpose and how important it was to his own. When Adam said, "she shall be called woman...", his statement concerning her was much deeper than Adam looking at her and saying, "Wo! Man." To be sure, the woman was beautiful. However, I believe that Adam's statement had more to do with who the woman was internally—a "womb-man"! When the Lord God brought the woman to Adam, in addition to seeing her external beauty, Adam discerned her internal value; he recognized that the Lord God had placed within the woman a womb—an avenue through which God's plan of fruitfulness and multiplication for Adam's life would be realized.

Adam was able to discern the woman's place and value both in and to his personal purpose and destiny; this is evident in what he said about her in Genesis 2:23. While the Lord God did bring the woman to Adam, what Adam said about her spoke to his accurate discernment of her, which allowed him to access the favor and grace that God was extending to him by and through the woman. As this was pertinent in Adam's case, it is also a divine pattern that will play a part in the destiny that God has established for every individual.

> Adam understood the woman's God-ordained role in his life. He recognized her make-up—*"bone of my bone and flesh of my flesh"*—as well as her purpose and how important it was to his own.

God will faithfully introduce us to the people who have a part/role in the destiny that He has determined for us. But, ultimately, it will be what "we say" about these individuals that will determine whether we access the favor and grace of God associated with these relationships. It's noteworthy that while the Lord God did bring the woman to Adam, nothing in Scripture indicates the Lord God forced their relationship. He did not force Adam to receive her. When the Lord God presented her to Adam, it was incumbent upon Adam to discern her and to determine her place in his life. This is a pattern and principle that shouldn't be taken lightly. In fact, God's plan for every person's life will involve God presenting unique people to him or her at critical times. While I've heard it said, "God will provide" more times and by more people than I can count, I often think these are words spoken by individuals who have not considered that perhaps people are God's greatest resource and provision. Although God will provide shelter, clothing, transportation, and so much more, *people* are more important to personal destiny than any other provision. *The fact that God brings the "right people" at the "right time" into our lives is an element upon which every person's destiny depends.* However, when God presents these individuals to us, He will not force them upon us; it will be our responsibility to recognize them and to properly assess their God-ordained place in our lives. This understanding has led to one of the most significant changes in my personal prayer life. In addition to the many things that I bring before God in prayer, I find myself constantly petitioning Him for the spiritual awareness to keenly and accurately discern people and their place in my life. Without this discernment, a person is essentially left with nothing to serve as a gauge for establishing the proper stewarding of the relationships in which they are involved—something that can be problematic or even detrimental.

> When God presents individuals to us, He will not force them upon us; it will be our responsibility to recognize them and to properly assess their God-ordained place in our lives.

While much can be said about the proper handling of the resources God has entrusted to us as stewards of His blessings, the significance of *properly* stewarding relationships, in my estimation, is not given *enough* attention. I raise this issue because in reading Genesis 2:15–20, it's apparent that Adam did well in stewarding the resources the Lord God gave him stewardship over in the Garden of Eden. Scripture indicates that Adam had no problem managing the Garden and its affairs; however, all of this was nullified due to Adam's mismanagement of his relationship with the woman. This is not to suggest God isn't honored or glorified by the proper stewarding of the things and resources He gives to a person's care and control; it is simply to point out that the lack of due regard for stewardship, in the area of personal relationship, is something that places a person's destiny in jeopardy. It is possible to manage situations and circumstances in a manner representative of exceptional stewardship but forfeit divine destiny through the mismanagement of personal relationships. The Bible clearly asserts it was Adam's failure in this area of his life that caused his downfall.

> *"...And the LORD God commanded the man, saying, of every tree of the garden thou mayest freely eat: but of the tree of the knowledge of good and evil, thou shalt not eat of it: for in the day that thou eatest thereof thou shalt surely die."* (Genesis 2:16–17)

> *"...And when the woman saw that the tree was good for food, and that it was pleasant to the eyes, and a tree to be desired to make one wise, she took of the fruit thereof, and did eat, and gave also unto her husband with her; and he did eat."* (Genesis 3:6)

These Scriptures specify that the Lord God's instructions to Adam concerning the trees of the Garden of Eden included a command *not* to eat of the tree of knowledge of good and evil (Genesis 2:16–17). Furthermore, they state that Adam's failure in eating from the forbidden tree was rooted in his failure in the area of personal relationship (Genesis 3:6). It was Adam's mishandling and lack of appropriate stewardship concerning his relationship with the woman that led Adam to eat from the forbidden tree, compromising their destiny. This compromise was, in large part, due to Adam's failure regarding *place*, a critical component of properly handling relationships.

Adam's fall was a direct result of satan's ability to cause a breach of

It is possible to manage situations and circumstances in a manner representative of exceptional stewardship but forfeit divine destiny through the mismanagement of personal relationships.

"place" concerning Adams's relationship with the woman. As I mentioned earlier, what Adam said about the woman was an indication he recognized her place in his life; and it was the woman's place that determined how she was to function. Though the woman had a significant role in Adam's life, her function did not include offering him something God had already determined to be off-limits and out of bounds. In this regard, the woman was out of place; however, the greater breach of place occurred with Adam. The Lord God gave him the command to "keep" (safeguard) the Garden (Genesis 2:15). This meant that once Adam recognized satan's deception in the woman's conversation with the serpent (Genesis 3:3–5), Adam's "place" dictated how he should have responded. Adam should have intervened. And by not taking the action associated with his place, Adam failed and satan gained the advantage.

> Though the woman did eat from the tree, God was more concerned with the fact that Adam ate. God's expectation of Adam was different from His expectation of the woman.

God's expectation of a person and the parameters that He establishes for that person's life are determined, in large part, by their God-ordained place.

When it comes to divine destiny, God's expectations are not the same for everyone. This is because the destiny that God has determined for a person's life will determine, to a great extent, how God designs that person to process information. Adam and his wife were both present during the conversation with the serpent in Genesis 3:6; however, they processed the situation totally different. Some have suggested the woman ate from the tree and then tricked Adam into doing the same. This was not the case. It is true the woman ate first, and she was instrumental in persuading Adam to eat as well, but Adam was in no way deceived by the woman, or the serpent for that matter, before eating from the tree. Adam ate and was fully aware of what he was doing and that his action was an act of rebellion against God. Truthfully, satan managed to deceive the woman, but Adam was not deceived.

> *"And Adam was not deceived, but the woman being deceived was in the transgression."* (1 Timothy 2:14)

This Scripture is an observation made by the apostle Paul about Adam and the woman eating from the tree of the knowledge of good and evil. Here, Paul makes it clear that the woman was deceived, but Adam transgressed. Though the woman did eat from the tree, God was more concerned with the fact that Adam ate. God's expectation of Adam was different from His expectation of the woman. This can be seen in God's response to their disobedience.

> *"And they heard the voice of the LORD God walking in the garden in the cool of the day and Adam and his wife hid themselves from the presence of the LORD God amongst the trees of the garden. And the LORD God called unto Adam and said unto him, Where art thou."* (Genesis 3:8–9)

These Scriptures clearly show that both Adam and his wife hid themselves from the presence of the Lord God because both had eaten. However, when the Lord God came to deal with the issue of disobedience, He called for Adam. This is because Adam was the one who received the commandment not to eat from the forbidden tree.

> *"And the LORD God took the man, and put him into the Garden of Eden to dress it and to keep it. And the LORD God commanded the man, saying, of every tree of the garden thou mayest freely eat: but of the tree of the knowledge of good and evil, thou shalt not eat of it: for in the day that thou eatest thereof thou shalt sure die."* (Genesis 2:15–17)

Scripture clearly indicates that the commandment not to eat of the tree of the knowledge of good and evil was given to Adam, not to the woman. As such, from God's perspective, it was Adam's place to steward the commandment. This became evident when God assigned blame and was even more evident in the consequences that followed Adam and the woman's disobedience.

> *"For as by one man's disobedience many were made sinners, so by the obedience of one shall many be made righteous."* (Romans 5:19)

From God's point of view, it was "one man"—not a couple—who caused humanity to fall into a state of sin, because it was Adam's place to steward the commandment. And the fact that it was the Lord God who made the woman and brought her to Adam did not lessen the severity of the consequences associated with Adam's disobedience. This should serve as a serious caution. While astute discernment relating to the people whom God will bring into our lives is something that has been stressed, understanding every individual's place in our lives is of utmost importance. This understanding will help to clarify, from God's vantage point, the expectations and the boundaries of the relationships in which we are involved. In fact, for people who are committed to realizing the destiny that God has ordained for their lives, it is beneficial to understand that "everyone has a place." In other words, every person whom God sends into our lives will be ordained to occupy a specific place in our lives. For those of us who may struggle with this concept of "place," it bears understanding that "place" speaks to *function*, not value.

Some people will read this book and associate place with personal value—which is a mistake. We are all of equal value to God. However, we were not all created to function the same way.

While I consider satan to be stupid on a good day, this has to do with the fact that as lucifer, he believed he could vanquish God—

take God's place; it has nothing to do with the craftiness he still possesses—craftiness that is very often effectively used to breach God's destiny and purpose in people's lives by causing violations of "place" in personal relationships. I believe one of the reasons why this has worked so effectively is because some people will read this book and associate place with personal value—which is a mistake. We are all of equal value to God. However, we were not all created to function the same way. There is no better example of this than God Himself. Each member of the God-Head has a unique place, and their respective place determines their distinct function. As mentioned earlier, the Father is God in creation, the Son is God in restoration, and the Holy Ghost is God in regeneration. Again, this is not to debate the Trinity of God. Rather, it is to point out that each person of the God-Head has a unique function, but any attempt to devalue any member by relegating Him to a place or status other than God is erroneous.

The ability to see the connection between place and function as it relates to relationships will be helpful in many ways. But perhaps, most importantly, it will keep us from making the mistake of trying to treat everyone the same way. While the word of God makes crystal clear the fact we are to treat everyone appropriately, as it relates to the destiny that God has determined for an individual's life, no biblical basis supports the notion that everyone with whom we are either "relational" or in "relationship" with should be treated the same way. This is simply *not scriptural.*

> In large part, our treatment of people—including our commitment to our relationship with them—should be commensurate with their God-ordained place in our lives.

In large part, our treatment of people—including our commitment to our relationship with them—should be commensurate with their God-ordained place in our lives. There is no better example of this reality than that of the Lord. During Jesus' earthly ministry, he did not treat everyone with whom He came into contact the same. I discuss this in greater detail later. For now, suffice it to say, if Jesus didn't treat everyone the same way, then anyone committed to the realization of God's destiny for his or her life should not attempt it either.

Surely, God is committed to the total fulfillment of the destiny He has established and ordained for every individual's life. However, seeing God's plan of destiny come to fruition will require the ability to discern the people associated with our destiny and to accurately determine their place in our life. This will not only help guard against being frustrated by people who don't live up to our expectations of them because God has not ordained them to be who we think or wish they were to us, it will also ensure we access the full potential of the grace and favor of God associated with those divinely orchestrated relationships that will prepare and propel us into our God-ordained destiny.

SECTION 1 STUDY QUESTIONS

1. Has this section affected your attitude about relationship(s)? If, so, How?

2. How much time did you devote to the proper discernment of people and relationships before reading this section?

3. Has reading this section changed your level of seriousness concerning adequately discerning people and their role(s) in your life? If so, how?

4. Has reading this section affected how you view stewardship when it comes to relationship(s)?

5. Did you find the author's position on "place" regarding relationship(s) helpful? Explain.

TIMES AND SEASONS

The conversation about discerning "times and seasons," as it relates to God's will for a person's life, often will primarily revolve around how circumstances and situations serve as indicators. While circumstances and situations can and will serve to identify God's desires for an individual's life at certain times and seasons, it would be more beneficial if *divinely orchestrated relationships* were a greater part of the "times and seasons" conversation. After the astute discernment of *circumstances* and *situations* associated with what God wants to communicate during given times and seasons, accessing the divine favor and grace that will be necessary to successfully navigate these periods will require keen discernment of *people* and *relationships*. Properly discerning "times and seasons" often necessitates the adequate discernment of God-ordained relationships. A prime example of this type of discernment is seen in the life of the prophet Elijah.

"And Elijah the Tishbite who was of the inhabitants of Gilead, said unto Ahab, as the LORD God of Israel liveth, before whom I stand, there shall not be dew nor rain these years, but according to my word. And the word of the LORD came unto him saying

get thee hence, and turn thee eastward and hide thyself by the brook Cherith that is before Jordan. And it shall be, that thou shalt drink of the brook: and I have commanded the ravens to feed thee there." (1 Kings 17:1–4)

"And it came to pass after a while, that the brook dried up, because there had been no rain in the land. And the word of the LORD came unto him, saying, Arise, get thee to Zarephath, which belongeth to Zidon, and dwell there: behold, I have commanded a widow woman there to sustain thee. So he arose and went to Zarephath. And when he came to the gate of the city, behold, the widow woman was there gathering of sticks: and he called to her, and said, Fetch me, I pray thee, a little water in a vessel, that I may drink. And as she was going to fetch it, he called to her, and said, Bring me, I pray thee, a morsel of bread in thine hand. And she said, As the LORD thy God liveth, I have not a cake, but an handful of meal in a barrel, and a little oil in a cruse: and, behold, I am gathering two sticks, that I may go in and dress it for me and my son, that we may eat it, and die." (1 Kings 17:7–12)

For a period during the three-and-a-half-year drought associated with the aforementioned Scriptures, God provided for Elijah by sending him to the Cherith brook from which Elijah drank water and ravens supplied him with food. A time came in the remainder of the season of drought, however, when God's provision for Elijah was connected to a God-ordained relationship. Although God told Elijah about a widow in Zarephath who was under divine command to sustain him, when Elijah encountered the woman, it was his responsibility to accurately discern her. This becomes evident as Elijah encounters the woman and does not immediately communicate to her what the Lord spoke to him at the brook.

I believe it was the woman's response to Elijah's request to bring him water and bread (1 Kings 17:10–11) that allowed him to recognize her as the person whom God would use to sustain him.

When Elijah posed a question, the woman's response was that she was about to prepare what she thought would be the last meal for her son and herself (1 Kings 17:12). Furthermore, when Elijah heard that the woman had a son, but she did not mention a husband, he recognized that the person with whom he was speaking was, in fact, the widow who was to sustain him. A point not to be overlooked is that even though the Lord told Elijah that He had commanded the widow to sustain him, upon their encounter her original plan was to eat her meal and die. It's clear the divine command to sustain Elijah was a mandate of which the widow was not aware. This was because it was Elijah's responsibility to *recognize her*. The widow had no responsibility in this regard. The reality is that divine destiny will often involve the ability to recognize the purpose for which God brings certain people into our lives before they are aware.

> Properly discerning "times and seasons" often necessitates the adequate discernment of God-ordained relationships.

When Elijah recognized the person with whom he was speaking was the widow who would sustain him, he spoke the word of the Lord to her.

> *"And Elijah said unto her, fear not; Go and do as thou has said: but make me thereof a little cake first, and bring it unto me, and after make for thee and thy son. For thus saith the LORD God, the barrel of meal shall not waste neither shall the cruse of oil fail, until the day that the LORD sendeth rain upon the earth."* (1 Kings 17:13–14)

These Scriptures show the Lord using the widow to make provision for Elijah; moreover, this requires Elijah to cultivate a relationship with the widow. That the relationship between Elijah and the woman is substantive is made very clear when reading the remainder of 1 Kings 17:15–24. This was a relationship that even included Elijah having living quarters in the loft of the widow's residence (1 Kings 17:19). Albeit, in the end, when the season of drought came to an end, the Lord spoke to Elijah and told him to go to another place.

> *"And it came to pass after many, days that the word of the LORD came to Elijah in the third year, saying, go shew thyself to Ahab; and I will send rain upon the earth."* (1 Kings 18:1)

The Bible does not mention if Elijah and the widow ever encounter each other again after he leaves her house; however, even if they did, their relationship would never have been the same because the season for which the Lord brought them together had ended. This will be the case in some of the relationships associated with God's destiny and purpose for every person's life.

> One of the greatest challenges to the successful navigation of divine relationship is realizing that many relationships will have a life cycle.

One of the greatest challenges to the successful navigation of divine relationship is realizing that many relationships, though ordained of God, will have a life cycle, which is not a dreadful thing. However, *not* understanding this will lead to the bad ending of many God-ordained relationships that were meant for good. Oftentimes, people who face "good relationship gone bad" challenges do so because they don't understanding the "times and seasons" of relationships.

As everyone travels the road that leads to their personal place of destiny, each person should understand that God's plan for fulfilling His purpose for their life will involve God orchestrating relationships with people that will include both entry and exit.

In other words, as we journey to our destiny, people will come and people will go—and this is not bad! "Hello's and goodbye's" are encounters God factors into the equation of every person's destiny. Accepting and being comfortable with this reality is something that will enable people to better navigate the divinely orchestrated relationships critical to their personal destiny. In this regard, we must understand that, in many cases, "hello" and "goodbye" are primarily associated with the relationship and not necessarily with the persons themselves. In other words, whether people are good or bad for us is not necessarily measured by how we may personally feel about them. When it comes to relationships involving God's purpose and destiny for a person's life, God is very intentional. God's intentionality can often lead to Him calling us into relationship with people for reasons other than what we might prefer or feel. As such, it is very beneficial to gauge our relationships by if and where people fit into the scope of God's plan of destiny for our lives. This is not an observation intended to suggest that being committed to

> God will generally bring people into our lives for one of three reasons: an event, a season, or destiny.

your destiny means everyone we encounter should be treated with some weird sense of spooky monitoring; it's only to point out that when it comes to divine destiny, we should be committed to "not" allowing our personal feelings—good or bad—about people to cause us to misdiagnose relationships. This requires not only keen discernment in the beginning as we identify those people who God sends into our lives, but it also requires us to consistently identify where we are in relation to the ordained life cycle of these relationships. It will not be the responsibility of the people who God brings into our lives to make these determinations. That responsibility is ours!

It helps to understand that when it comes to times and seasons associated with the fulfillment of divine purpose, God will generally bring people into our lives for one of three reasons: an event, a season, or destiny. The successful navigation of the relationships

God orchestrates will demand an understanding that not everyone whom God brings into our lives will always be a part of our lives. Many relationships associated with our destiny will involve people whom God will use to significantly impact our lives, but our relationships with them will be ordained for a specific event or particular season. In such cases, it is vital to understand that the grace and favor of God associated with these relationships are only good until either the "event" is over or the "season" has ended.

It is also of great benefit to understand there will be instances when staying in step with God's plan of destiny will require discerning, with great precision, when the divine purpose for certain relationships has been served. Not recognizing or understanding this is why, I believe, many relationships that are ordained of God for inspiration and/or impartation end with animosity, anger, hurt, or other negative feelings. Too often, relationships that were meant to bring God glory end badly and leave those involved feeling betrayed. The truth of the matter is that, in many of these instances, the issue

> Staying in step with God's plan of destiny will require discerning, with great precision, when the divine purpose for certain relationships has been served.

is not betrayal—the issue is *extension of relationships beyond their God-ordained life cycle.* My intent is not to suggest that legitimate cases of betrayal never occur; rather, my aim is to point out that God's plan of destiny for a person's life will, in some instances, mean that once God's objective has been accomplished, for all intents and purposes, the relationship is over.

To reiterate, when the season for which God orchestrated the relationship between Elijah and the widow had ended, *Elijah moved on!* This is a practice that should be incorporated into the life of anyone committed to the fulfillment of their destiny. It will not always feel good, but it will be beneficial.

God's plan of destiny for everyone's life will include relationships with ordained life cycles. Acceptance of this reality will better prepare people to successfully recognize and navigate the "times and seasons" associated with God-ordained relationships.

SECTION 2 STUDY QUESTIONS

1. On a scale of 1 -10, how helpful did you find the authors position on "times and seasons" of relationships? Explain.

2. Has reading this section affected your view with regard to people exiting your life? If so, how?

3. What was your comfort level regarding people exiting your life prior to reading this section? What is it now?

4. Can you identify a relationship that you attempted to extend beyond its God-ordained life cycle? How will you guard against this in the future?

MENTORS MATTER

In recent years, a more robust dialogue has revolved around the value of mentors. The conversation about the importance of mentorship is one that appears to be leading many to understand how valuable mentors are to the process associated with the fulfillment of a person's destiny. In other words, more people are coming to understand and accept the fact that, as it pertains to divine destiny, mentors matter. Mentorship can mean a lot of things to a lot of people, it is a topic that is getting quite a bit of attention in both "sacred' and "secular" arenas. While sacred principles will work in secular settings, we must understand that just because something works does not mean that God has committed to its fulfillment. God will only commit to the fulfillment of what He establishes or ordains. My desire is to highlight the importance of having, and God's faithfulness in providing mentors as it relates to fulfilling the destiny God ordains and establishes for our lives. We have already highlighted the importance of discerning people and their place regarding our destiny; albeit, when it comes to the proper discernment of divinely orchestrated relationships, though each relationship is significant, *recognizing* mentors should be a high priority in the life of anyone committed to seeing God's plan of destiny fulfilled in his or her life. The fact that mentors are an essential part of God's ordained destiny and purpose for an individual's life is evidenced throughout the Bible. While their vastness will not permit me to give attention to all of the mentor-mentee relationships contained in Scripture, two of God's most notable servants are fitting examples: Moses and Samuel. The Bible clearly illustrates *how* God felt about His relationship with both of these men.

> *"Then said the LORD unto me, though Moses and Samuel stood before me, yet my mind could not be toward this people: cast them out of my sight, and let them go forth."* (Jeremiah 15:1)

In this Scripture passage, the Lord was responding to the request of the prophet Jeremiah to turn from the judgment that the Lord had determined to bring against Judah (Jeremiah 14:17–22). The Lord's response to Jeremiah's plea, though not favorable for Judah, did illustrate the Lord's feelings about the relationship that He had with Moses and Samuel. The Lord was saying that if Moses and Samuel could not cause Him to stay His judgment in this matter, then no one could. It is evident in the Word of God that Moses and Samuel were favored of God.

The mentors who God sends into our lives will often be different from us.

There are numerous Scriptures in which the Lord's pleasure with the life of Moses and Samuel shines through. And while we can't dispute that Moses and Samuel were choice servants of the Lord, that God used mentors to provide counsel and guidance to them as it related to their divine assignments and destiny is also noted in Scripture.

> *"And Moses' father in law said unto him, The thing that thou doest is not good. Thou wilt surely wear away, both thou, and this people that is with thee: for this thing is*

too heavy for thee; thou art not able to perform it thyself alone. Hearken now unto my voice, I will give thee counsel, and God shall be with thee: Be thou for the people to God-ward, that thou mayest bring the causes unto God: And thou shalt teach them ordinances and laws, and shalt shew them the way wherein they must walk, and the work that they must do. Moreover thou shalt provide out of all the people able men, such as fear God, men of truth, hating covetousness; and place such over them, to be rulers of thousands, and rulers of hundreds, rulers of fifties, and rulers of tens: And let them judge the people at all seasons: and it shall be, that every great matter they shall bring unto thee, but every small matter they shall judge: so shall it be easier for thyself, and they shall bear the burden with thee. If thou shalt do this thing, and God command thee so, then thou shalt be able to endure, and all these people shall also go to their place in peace. So Moses hearkened to the voice of his father in law, and did all that he had said. And Moses chose able men out of all Israel, and made them heads over the people, rulers of thousands, rulers of hundreds, rulers of fifties, and rulers of tens. And they judged the people at all seasons: the hard causes they brought unto Moses, but every small matter they judged themselves." (Exodus 18:17–26)

With all the exploits the Lord used Moses to perform in delivering the children of Israel from Egyptian bondage, Jethro recognized that Moses' style of leadership, if continued, would ultimately prove to be too burdensome for Moses—as well as for the children of Israel—and would produce disastrous results. Moses accepted Jethro's counsel, and it proved beneficial for both Moses and the nation of Israel. Worth noting is the fact that Moses was willing to *hear* Jethro, even after being used so mightily of the Lord to bring the people of Israel out of Egypt. Also noteworthy is that Jethro was a Midianite. Midianites, though thought to be descendants of Abraham, had no part in Israel's promised inheritance. While some scholars theorize they may have retained some expressions that acknowledged the God of Abraham, Midianites were idolaters, and so was Jethro (Exodus 18:11). In this respect, Jethro was not like Moses. I make this observation as both counsel and caution: the mentors who God sends into our lives will often be different from us. If God used an idolater to provide mentorship to Moses, then shame on the person who fails to discern his mentors simply because they are of a different race, socio-economic class, political party, denominational affiliation, or any other difference. For people who are ordained to make a significant impact in this world, divine destiny will include times and seasons in which their perspective will have to be broadened—perspective that, in some cases, will only come through people who are not "just like us."

We'll next look at Samuel. Previously, I alluded to the importance of mentors regardless of a person's age and/or level of experience. Samuel helps to illustrate the significance of this point in great contrast to Moses as it relates to Samuel's age and level of experience when God connected Samuel to his mentor, Eli.

> *"And when she had weaned him, she took him up with her, with three bullocks, and one ephah of flour, and a bottle of wine, and brought him unto the house of the* LORD *in Shiloh: and the child was young. And they slew a bullock, and brought the child to Eli."* (1 Samuel 1:24–25)

When Jethro came to Moses from Midian, Moses was already 80 (plus) years old and experienced regarding his divine assignment. In contrast, as stated in the preceding Scripture, the Lord orchestrated circumstances in Samuel's life that, as a child, he was placed in the care of Eli. Something I find very informative about this divinely orchestrated mentor-mentee relationship is that, although Eli was a high priest, he was not perfect. Eli's flaws are clearly recognizable in 1 Samuel 2:12–36. Scripture bears out that Eli was not a perfect priest, nor was he the perfect parent. However, God

determined that Eli would mentor Samuel, who would function not only as a priest but also as a judge and one of the most notable prophets of the nation of Israel. When it comes to the consideration of mentorship, this should serve as a valuable lesson. Mentors will not be perfect people. However, *as it relates to accomplishing the will and purpose for which God brings them into someone's life, mentors will be the perfect people for the task.* This does not mean that we should not look for character, integrity, and honesty in a mentor. It is only meant to point out that, though a good mentor should possess the qualities, traits, and characteristics associated with people we hold in high esteem, they will not be perfect.

Staying focused on the *reason* that God brings mentors into our lives will mean, in all probability, setting aside some things about them that may not sit well with us personally—things that have absolutely nothing to do with either the purpose for which God brought them into our lives or their ability to fulfill their God-ordained assignment.

> Mentors will not be perfect people. However, *as it relates to accomplishing the will and purpose for which God brings them into someone's life, mentors will be the perfect people for the task*

Though flawed, Eli taught Samuel things about the priesthood and other areas of service unto the Lord that were vital to Samuel's development and his ability to discharge the duties associated with the office in which the Lord ordained him to serve. In fact, it was Eli who instructed Samuel in how to respond to the call of God.

"That the LORD called Samuel: and he answered, Here am I. And he ran unto Eli, and said, Here am I; for thou calledst me. And he said, I called not; lie down again.

*And he went and lay down. And the LORD called yet
again, Samuel. And Samuel arose and went to Eli, and
said, Here am I; for thou didst call me. And he answered,
I called not, my son; lie down again. Now Samuel did
not yet know the LORD, neither was the word of the LORD
yet revealed unto him. And the LORD called Samuel
again the third time. And he arose and went to Eli, and
said, Here am I; for thou didst call me. And Eli perceived
that the LORD had called the child. Therefore Eli said
unto Samuel, Go, lie down: and it shall be, if he call thee,
that thou shalt say, Speak, LORD; for thy servant heareth.
So Samuel went and lay down in his place. And the LORD
came, and stood, and called as at other times, Samuel,
Samuel. Then Samuel answered, Speak; for thy servant
heareth. And the LORD said to Samuel, Behold, I will do
a thing in Israel, at which both the ears of every one that
heareth it shall tingle."* (1 Samuel 3:4–11)

Here, the Word of God reveals that when the Lord called Samuel,
he did not recognize the Lord's voice. Samuel thought the voice
he heard was Eli's and responded by going to Eli three times. Finally, Eli perceived it was the Lord who called Samuel, so Eli then
instructed Samuel on how to respond. When Samuel responded
in the way Eli instructed, the Lord proceeded to reveal Himself
to Samuel as the Lord desired. Some suggest the take-away from
these Scriptures is that to Samuel, God sounded like Eli. In contrast, others go to great lengths to disprove this notion. No one
can say with absolute certainty which position is right. On the
other hand, no one can dispute the fact it was the instruction Samuel received from Eli that positioned him for the Lord to begin to
use him in a manner reflective of His divine purpose and personal
destiny for Samuel.

The Bible paints a very clear picture of the importance of mentors.
In fact, when it comes to divine destiny, mentors are necessary and
their value, immeasurable. For anyone to believe he can access all

that God has determined for his life without godly counsel, guidance, or wisdom from mentors is a mistake. While everyone can appreciate a "rags to riches" story in which someone beats the odds and succeeds through dedication, hard work and commitment, when it comes to divine destiny, regardless of what that may be or how it might look, no one will ever be "self-made."

SECTION 3 STUDY QUESTIONS

1. On a scale of 1 – 10, how would you have rated the value of mentors before reading this section? How would you rate them now?

2. Who has mentored you in the past? How have they impacted your life?

3. Do you have a mentor now? If so, who is it and how are they contributing to your life?

4. If you do not have a mentor, will you seek one? Who might this be?

5. How open are you to mentoring others?

6. Are you intentionally mentoring others? Why or why not?

THE BLESSINGS OF SPIRITUAL FATHERS

In addition to mentoring, the concept of spiritual fathering is receiving a great deal of attention. Though the term "spiritual father" is not found in Scripture, I believe the profound depth and intimacy associated with the term "father"—as it is used in association with those responsible for the spiritual formation and development of the people they were ordained to prepare for destiny—is something that explains and validates the concept. For people who would ask, "Aren't mentors and spiritual fathers one and the same?" my answer is, "Not necessarily." While all spiritual fathers will be mentors, not all mentors will be spiritual fathers. Though there are numerous differences between the roles of mentors and spiritual fathers, one of the most noticeable differences in Scripture can be reduced to two words: "information" and "example."

In relation to divine destiny, mentors provide much needed information while spiritual fathers will provide a much-needed example—an example meant or ordained to prepare people for divine destiny in ways that no other relationship can accomplish.

The depth of the relationship with a spiritual father will be greater than that of a mentor, largely due to the impartation that a spiritual father will make as a part of the spiritual formation needed in a person's life to fulfill the destiny that God has established for that person. This is something the relationship between Elijah and Elisha clearly illustrates.

> *"And it came to pass, when the LORD would take up Elijah into heaven by a whirlwind, that Elijah went with Elisha from Gilgal."* (2 Kings 2:1)

> *"And Elijah took his mantle, and wrapped it together, and smote the waters, and they were divided hither and thither, so that they two went over on dry ground. And it came to pass, when they were gone over, that Elijah said unto Elisha, Ask what I shall do for thee, before I be taken away from thee. And Elisha said, I pray thee, let a double portion of thy spirit be upon me. And he said, Thou hast asked a hard thing: nevertheless, if thou see me when I am taken from thee, it shall be so unto thee; but if not, it shall not be so. And it came to pass, as they still went on, and talked, that, behold, there appeared a chariot of fire, and horses of fire, and parted them both asunder; and Elijah went up by a whirlwind into heaven. And Elisha saw it, and he cried, My father, my father, the chariot of Israel, and the horsemen thereof. And he saw him no more: and he took hold of his own clothes, and rent them in two pieces. He took up also the mantle of Elijah that fell from him, and went back, and stood by the bank of Jordan; And he took the mantle of Elijah that fell from him, and smote the waters, and said, Where is the LORD God of Elijah? and when he also had smitten the waters,*

they parted hither and thither: and Elisha went over." (2 Kings 2:8–14)

Here, we see an account of the events that surround Elijah being taken into heaven. These verses of Scripture are often used to call attention to the fact that the Bible credits Elisha with twice the number of miracles than those performed by Elijah—32 to 16. It is often suggested that the 32 miracles credited to Elisha were the result of him receiving double the measure or amount of the Spirit of God that was upon Elijah when he was taken into heaven. 2 Kings 2:9 is used to validate this point by treating Elisha's request for a "double portion" of Elijah's spirit to be upon him as though Elisha was asking to receive twice the measure or amount of the Spirit of God that was upon Elijah. However, that this is erroneous is fairly easy to see when noting that, as it relates to Elisha's request in that particular passage of Scripture, the word "spirit" is spelled with a lower case "s" which underscores the fact this was not a reference to the Spirit of God. Had Elisha been referring to the Holy Spirit, the "s" would have been capitalized. Understanding this gives a better understanding of the nature of Elisha's request to have a "double portion" of Elijah's spirit. In essence, Elisha's request was an expression of his desire to be "twice the man" he found Elijah to be. Elisha saw Elijah as a man worth following (2 Kings 2:2–6).

> Mentors provide much needed information while spiritual fathers will provide a much-needed example.

While mentors will provide *instructions* worth following, spiritual fathers will be *people* worth following. Though they will provide information and instruction, spiritual fathers will also greatly contribute to a person's spiritual formation and development by way of "spiritual impartation," which will flow, in large part, out of who they are as spiritual fathers. A spiritual father will, in many cases, provide an individual with the personal example needed for that person to access and properly steward many of the *spiritual things* associated with his or her destiny. Spiritual fathers teach people things about God that will never be accessed in a book, a classroom, or online. This is certainly not a knock against any of these, as they are all valuable methods of learning and instruction. When it comes to divine destiny, however, anyone who has ever had an authentic relationship with a spiritual father would attest to the fact that things gleaned from books, classrooms, and the Internet, while helpful, cannot be compared to the value of a God-ordained relationship with a true spiritual father.

Spiritual fathers provide for the production of spiritual stability and effectiveness, and they teach the lessons associated with the spiritual disciplines needed for a person to fulfill God's ordained destiny for his or her life. Also, by way of example, they provide a framework for the application and life strategy—applying and living out—of the things they impart. The two most important things that Elijah provided for Elisha was a "spiritual example" and a "spiritual impartation." These were the things that impacted Elisha's life such that his desire was to simply be "twice the man" that he found Elijah to be. I believe this also triggered Elisha's reference to Elijah as he was taken away: "My father, my father, the chariot of Israel…" (2 Kings 2:12). This also leads to an interesting point—what Elisha *did not say* when Elijah was taken away. Elisha did not say, "I see you." Instead, he said, "My father, my father, the chariot of Israel…" I believe this reference to Elijah is interesting and can serve to teach a great lesson about the importance of a person's ability to accurately discern people.

When Elisha asked to receive a double portion of Elijah's spirit, Elijah responded, "Thou hath asked a hard thing: nevertheless, if thou see me when I am taken away from thee, it shall be so unto thee; but if not, it shall not be so" (2 Kings 2:9–10). Elisha's response when Elijah was taken away—not "I see you" but rather "My father, my father, the chariot of Israel…"—indicates Elijah's statement to Elisha about seeing Elijah was a challenge that had more to do with recognition than visibility. In other words, the determining factor concerning Elisha's request was not his ability to physically see Elijah; it was if Elisha was able to spiritually discern who Elijah was to Elisha personally and to Israel as a nation. And that Elisha went on to do twice as much as Elijah, in a sense, serves as a clear indication that Elisha's request was granted. Elijah's statement about whether or not Elisha would receive a double portion of his spirit seems to suggest that the decision was Elijah's to make. This is something that has caused tension regarding the power of one person to dictate the release of spiritual authority to someone else. While I don't profess to be an expert concerning this particular matter, I have come to understand that the relationship between Elijah and Elisha may serve to bring a greater level of clarity to "the transfer of spiritual authority" concept. In my opinion, all spiritual authority comes from God. I believe no one has the power to release spiritual authority to someone else in and of themselves. That said, I also believe God orchestrates relationships in which certain people are ordained and empowered by God to facilitate the release of spiritual authority to other people. Although the spiritual authority will come *from* God ultimately, it will be accessed through the relationships that He uses to prepare and equip the people to whom the spiritual authority is to be released. Elijah and Elisha

> Spiritual fathers provide for the production of spiritual stability and effectiveness, and they teach the lessons associated with the spiritual disciplines needed for a person to fulfill God's ordained destiny for his or her life.

provide a great illustration of this spiritual dynamic. While Elijah, in and of himself, did not have the authority to do anything of spiritual significance for Elisha, by virtue of the fact that God ordained Elijah to prepare and equip Elisha for his divine assignment and destiny, the spiritual authority associated with Elisha's destiny, though it came from God, was released in his life through his relationship with Elijah. Elisha's recognition of the significance of this spiritual dynamic is something that can be seen when considering what he said in the working of his first recorded miracle in Scripture.

> *"And he took the mantle of Elijah that fell from him, and smote the waters, and said, Where is the LORD God of Elijah? and when he also had smitten the waters, they parted hither and thither and Elisha went over."* (2 Kings 2:14)

In Elisha's remarks, a valuable lesson can be learned about the vital role people who serve as spiritual fathers can play as it relates to the releasing of spiritual authority in another person's life. When Elisha said, "Where is the Lord God of Elijah?" he made a statement that honored the Lord by acknowledging Elijah, the person whom the Lord ordained to prepare and equip Elisha for the destiny that God established for him. Contained in what Elisha said was an expression of his appreciation for his relationship with the person who had taught him so much about the Lord and had been such an example to him.

In my opinion, all spiritual authority comes from God. That said, I also believe God orchestrates relationships in which certain people are ordained and empowered by God to facilitate the release of spiritual authority to other people.

Immediately after Elijah is taken away, the significance of his example and impartation in Elisha's life and ministry becomes clear in Scripture. Before Elijah and Elisha crossed the Jordan River, Elisha observed Elijah smite the waters with his mantle and the waters were divided (2 Kings 2:8). Once Elijah was taken and it was time for Elisha to return, he took Elijah's mantle and did exactly what he had seen Elijah do—with the same result. The Lord did for Elisha what He had already and "recently" done for Elijah. The parting of the Jordan River as a "recent" occurrence at this point in the life and ministry of Elijah is worth noting because it highlights what is, in my opinion, one of the most important spiritual dynamics associated with the success of Elisha's ministry—Elijah's last miracle was Elisha's first miracle; Elisha started where Elijah finished. This was a true indication of the parent's ceiling being the protégé's floor. While I have a great appreciation for the ways in which the Lord used Elisha, I must point out that Elijah's example and impartation was a necessary part of the spiritual journey that prepared Elisha for his destiny and success. While the Bible does credit Elisha with twice the number of

> The ways in which the Lord's power was manifested in Elisha's life and ministry serve as a great lesson in the illustration of the value and validity of the transfer of spiritual authority in divinely orchestrated spiritual father-son relationships.

miracles attributed to Elijah, the role that Elijah played in preparing Elisha for his destiny speaks volumes to the value of a divinely orchestrated relationship with a spiritual father. The ways in which the Lord's power was manifested in Elisha's life and ministry serve as a great lesson in the illustration of the value and validity of the transfer of spiritual authority in divinely orchestrated spiritual father-son relationships. That the relationship between Elijah and Elisha was one in which the spiritual authority that was present in

Elijah's life and ministry was transferred and released in the life and ministry of Elisha is further evident when the sons of the prophets at Jericho observed Elisha after he crossed the Jordan with Elijah and then returned. They recognized that the spirit of Elijah was on Elisha.

> *"And when the sons of the prophets which were to view at Jericho saw him, they said, The spirit of Elijah doth rest on Elisha. And they came to meet him, and bowed themselves to the ground before him."* (2 Kings 2:15)

For anyone who understands that their destiny will require substantial spiritual formation and preparation, the role Elijah played in preparing Elisha for his destiny is something that can serve to illustrate that when it comes to the spiritual dynamics and lessons associated with divine destiny, a divinely orchestrated relationship with a spiritual father will be of great benefit.

The relationship between Elijah and Elisha provides a sound illustration of the effectiveness and spiritual value of a spiritual father-son relationship. Without question, the example and impartation that Elijah provided for Elisha yielded substantial fruit in Elisha's life. As I mentioned previously, I believe Elisha received the "double portion" he desired, which is evidenced by the Bible attributing to Elisha twice the number of miracles attributed to Elijah. While this is noteworthy as it relates to the impact that Elijah had on Elisha's life, often overlooked is the broader impact of Elijah's investment.

In addition to the miracles attributed to Elisha, the Bible also gives a clear but often overlooked picture of the impact that Elisha made in the lives of the "sons of the prophets" (2 Kings 2:3,5,7, 14–15, 4:38–41, 6:1–7, 9:1–6). Understanding who the sons of the prophets were sheds light on the broader impact of Elijah's investment in Elisha's life. The individuals referenced in these Scripture verses were not called "sons of the prophets" because their natural fathers were prophets. The sons of the prophets were young men who showed spiritual promise and were gathered together to be prepared for ministry. The term "sons of the prophets" was given to them as an expression of both their "spiritual promise" and their "spiritual immaturity." Once again, a careful reading of Scriptures can give a clear picture of the significant role Elisha played in teaching these young men the spiritual lessons associated with their destiny, as well as the importance of Elisha's example and impartation in their lives. The vital role that Elisha played in preparing the sons of the prophets was an essential part of their spiritual growth and development, and there is no question that Elisha prepared the sons of the prophets well. What is also unquestionable is that many of the things that Elisha did before—and imparted to—the sons of the prophets were things he learned and received through the life and ministry of Elijah. That Elijah prepared Elisha well is documented in Scripture. The 2 to 1 ratio of miracles speaks to this fact and is unmistakable evidence of the impact and value of Elijah's investment in Elisha's life and ministry. However, I believe the broader and, perhaps, greater impact and value of Elijah's investment in Elisha's life and ministry can be seen in that the things Elisha learned from Elijah not only prepared him for his personal destiny but also enabled him to prepare others for the destiny that the Lord ordained for their lives. The example and impartation that Elisha provided to the sons of the prophets after Elijah was taken speaks to this truth. The Bible clearly communicates Elisha's role and ability to prepare the sons of the prophets for the destiny that the Lord ordained for their life.

> *And Elisha came again to Gilgal: and there was a dearth in the land; and the sons of the prophets were sitting before him: and he said unto his servant, Set on the great pot, and seethe pottage for the sons of the prophets. And one went out into the field to gather herbs, and found a wild vine, and gathered thereof wild gourds his lap full, and came and shred them into the pot of pottage: for they knew them not. So they poured out for the men to eat. And it came to pass, as they were eating of the pottage,*

that they cried out, and said, O thou man of God, there is death in the pot. And they could not eat thereof. But he said, Then bring meal. And he cast it into the pot; and he said, Pour out for the people, that they may eat. And there was no harm in the pot." (2 Kings 4:38–41)

"And the sons of the prophets said unto Elisha, Behold now, the place where we dwell with thee is too strait for us. Let us go, we pray thee, unto Jordan, and take thence every man a beam, and let us make us a place there, where we may dwell. And he answered, Go ye. And one said, Be content, I pray thee, and go with thy servants. And he answered, I will go. So he went with them. And when they came to Jordan, they cut down wood. But as one was felling a beam, the axe head fell into the water: and he cried, and said, Alas, master! for it was borrowed. And the man of God said, Where fell it? And he shewed him the place. And he cut down a stick, and cast it in thither; and the iron did swim. Therefore said he, Take it up to thee. And he put out his hand, and took it." (2 Kings 6:1–7)

"And Elisha the prophet called one of the children of the prophets, and said unto him, Gird up thy loins, and take this box of oil in thine hand, and go to Ramothgilead: And when thou comest thither, look out there Jehu the son of Jehoshaphat the son of Nimshi, and go in, and make him arise up from among his brethren, and carry him to an inner chamber; Then take the box of oil, and pour it on his head, and say, Thus saith the LORD, I have anointed thee king over Israel. Then open the door, and flee, and tarry not." (2 Kings 9:1–3)

Detailed in these passages is the vital role that Elisha played in preparing the sons of the prophets for their destiny and purpose. The example and impartation that Elisha provided to the sons of the prophets is illuminated here. However, something not as apparent but significant is that many of the spiritual lessons Elisha taught the sons of the prophets were lessons he learned from Elijah. To be sure, much of what the sons of the prophets received from their relationship with Elisha was due to Elisha's relationship with Elijah. And while we know the number of miracles the Bible attributes to both Elijah and Elisha, none of us know how many miracles the sons of the prophets—individually or collectively—went on to perform after having been taught the spiritual lessons they learned from Elisha. I have a great deal of appreciation for the roles and functions of spiritual fathers and not solely for the personal impact that a spiritual father's investment will have in the lives of the people whom they are ordained to prepare for divine destiny. I appreciate the broader impact of their investment.

While Elisha's relationship with Elijah led to Elisha receiving the "double portion" he requested (2 Kings 2:9) and working double the number of miracles than his spiritual father worked, it was Elijah's investment in Elisha's life that prepared Elisha in such a way that he was able to prepare others. This investment is something that can serve to help better understand and appreciate the impact and value of the spiritual preparation provided by those individuals who are truly ordained of the Lord to function and serve as spiritual fathers.

As already mentioned, I view the primary function and role of spiritual fathers as providing a "spiritual" example and impartation associated with the spiritual formation and development of others. This is clearly illustrated through the life and writings of the apostle Paul.

> *"For I long to see you, that I may impart unto you some spiritual gift, to the end ye may be established;"* (Romans 1:11)

"Be ye followers of me, even as I also am of Christ." (1 Corinthians 11:1)

Paul understood his role to be one of providing people whose lives he touched with a "spiritual impartation and example" as illustrated in the preceding Scriptures. In Romans 1:11, Paul expresses his desire to "impart some spiritual gift," and in 1 Corinthians 11:1, he challenges members of the church at Corinth to "follow him," which was a reference to his example to them. Paul's desire was not that the Corinthians fall in behind him and follow him physically. It was, rather, that they would follow the spiritual example that he set. In 1 Corinthians 11:1, we find Paul communicating that message as it relates to following Christ. Paul had lived before the members of the church at Corinth in a manner that provided them with an example worthy of imitation. These Scripture references (Romans 1:11; 1 Corinthians 11:1) clearly indicate that Paul viewed providing people with a "spiritual" example and impartation as a part of his divine assignment. Moreover, Scripture clearly communicates that Paul took the role of providing for the spiritual formation of others very seriously.

> Paul's desire was not that the Corinthians fall in behind him and follow him physically. It was, rather, that they would follow the spiritual example that he set.

"My little children, of whom I travail in birth again until Christ be formed in you..." (Galatians 4:19)

A spiritual father's role will primarily involve the spiritual formation that needs to take place in people's lives for them to fulfill the destiny and purpose God ordains for them. Galatians 4:19 speaks to Paul's desire and commitment to seeing spiritual formation realized in the lives of those who were a part of the church at Galatia.

The preceding verse begins with Paul referring to them as "my little children," which indicates Paul is addressing them from the place and position of a spiritual father, whose primary concern is their spiritual growth and development. In discerning whether the Lord has given someone to serve as a spiritual father, it is of great benefit to first understand that the Lord gives spiritual fathers for spiritual reasons. Although a true spiritual father can, and most often will, be helpful in many areas of life, in order to access the full favor and grace of God that comes by and through relationships with spiritual fathers, it is important to grasp their function and role. The Lord does not bring spiritual fathers into people's lives to tell them what food to eat, car to drive, clothes to wear, home to purchase, or other such matters. While the things mentioned are areas in which a spiritual father may be knowledgeable enough to offer helpful advice, none of these represent the purpose for which the Lord sends spiritual fathers into people's lives. As it relates to any of the aforementioned areas, the Lord can, has, and will continue to provide people with the information they need through relationships that are a lot less meaningful than a relationship with a spiritual father.

A spiritual father's role will primarily involve the spiritual formation that needs to take place in people's lives for them to fulfill the destiny and purpose God ordains for them.

Relationships with spiritual fathers will most often prove to be beneficial in many areas of a person's life; however, understanding that a spiritual father's primary function will involve spiritual formation will help people to properly discern when the Lord has sent a spiritual father into their lives and to understand the spiritual father's place and role. While some have viewed the concept of spiritual fathers with skepticism, and others have rejected the concept altogether, I believe much of this skepticism and rejection is due to people's lack of understanding that, as it relates to divinely ordained and orchestrated relationships, the term "spiritual father" involves *function* not *title!* Such understanding makes it easy to reconcile what Jesus said in Matthew, Chapter 23 with what Paul communicates in 1 Corinthians, Chapter 4.

> *"And call no man your father upon the earth: for one is your Father, which is in heaven."* (Matthew 23:9)

> *"For though ye have ten thousand instructors in Christ, yet have ye not many fathers: for in Christ Jesus I have begotten you through the gospel. Wherefore I beseech you, be ye followers of me. For this cause have I sent unto you Timotheus, who is my beloved son, and faithful in the LORD, who shall bring you into remembrance of my ways which be in Christ, as I teach everywhere in every church."* (1 Corinthians 4:15–17)

In Matthew 23:9, it is easy to see that Jesus' teaching had to do with *men* being called *father*. In 1 Corinthians 4:15–17, there is no indication that Paul sought to be referred to as *father*. In fact, there is no evidence in any of Paul's writings that he ever sought to be called *father*, and nothing in Scripture suggests that anyone ever used the title "father" when referring to Paul. While this is not an attempt to debate the "call no man father" issue, it should be noted that when Paul alluded to himself as a father in Scripture, it had nothing to do with his title; it was from the vantage point of role and responsibility. In 1 Corinthians, Chapter 4, Paul makes it clear that his relationship with the people who were a part of the church at Corinth was very different

> Understanding that a spiritual father's primary function will involve spiritual formation will help people to properly discern when the Lord has sent a spiritual father into their lives.

from that of an instructor (1 Corinthians 4:15). He points out that his role and responsibility as a spiritual father brought along with it a greater level of commitment to the Corinthian's spiritual growth, development, and well-being. It's important to understand that when Paul alluded to himself as a father in this verse of Scripture, it was not to suggest the things the Corinthians learned from instructors were of no value. It was meant, however, to point out that Paul's role and responsibility as a spiritual father was different than that of an instructor. Paul's use of the term "instructors" in verse 15 serves to illustrate his understanding of their value; "instructors" in the aforementioned verse is derived from the Greek word "paidagogos," which refers to the person who conducted the children from home to school. Though the term "paidagogos" is not easy to accurately translate because we do not have a similar role in American culture, its meaning is very similar to the role of a nanny, but with much more teaching responsibility. Those who served in the role to which Paul was referring when he used the term "instructors" in 1 Corinthians 4:15 were trusted slaves who served as guardians and into whose care fathers turned over their children. There was a robust mentoring component to the guardians' function as they tutored children, taught them good manners, and looked out for them in general. Though the guardians had a very important role in the children's development, the guardian's role never replaced the role of the father. In this verse of Scripture, Paul is communicating to the Corinthians that an instructor's place in their lives was very different than the "place" Paul held with them as their spiritual father. Paul spoke to the reality of this concept in his letter to the church at Galatia in Galatians 4:1–2.

> *"Now I say, That the heir, as long as he is a child, differeth nothing from a servant, though he be Lord of all; But is under tutors and governors until the time appointed of the father."* (Galatians 4:1–2)

Likewise, Paul's place with the Corinthians was unique because it was through this preaching that the Corinthians came to the faith in Jesus Christ. And while it has been suggested that this was the only legitimate basis for Paul's reference to himself as a father, it is clear that Paul is not addressing those who are a part of the church at Corinth from the place of an evangelist who, through the preaching of Jesus, the Corinthians came to faith in Jesus Christ. Although this *was* the case (Paul did function as an evangelist to the Corinthians). Paul was speaking from the place of a spiritual father with a profound sense of responsibility for the spiritual growth, development, and well-being of the Corinthians. While Paul *did* function as both evangelist and spiritual father to the people who came to know Jesus Christ through his ministry, it should be understood that, although a person is a great evangelist and used of God in winning many people to the Lord, it does not necessarily mean they are to serve as a spiritual father to those people.

The person whom God uses to bring an individual to acknowledging Jesus as Lord and Savior will very often be a different person than the spiritual father who is ordained to provide the spiritual example and impartation regarding the spiritual formation associated with that individual's God-ordained destiny. I am personally acquainted with this reality since the person who led me to give my life to Jesus was not the individual who served as the spiritual father who taught me the much-needed spiritual disciplines and lessons that were a part of the spiritual formation that took place in my life after I accepted Jesus as Lord and Savior. I am very thankful to the brother who led me to faith in Jesus Christ. Even so, the truth is, even though he led me, one-on-one, in pray-

> As it relates to divinely ordained and orchestrated relationships, the term "spiritual fathers" involves *function not title!*

ing the prayer of repentance, I don't remember his name. However, I will never forget the spiritual father who taught me to pray, challenged me to fast, stressed the importance of "searching the Scriptures," encouraged me when I felt intimidated, and made demands of me when I was resistant to the Lord's will—all with the constant challenge of "Get to know Him for yourself."

While I am the first to admit I have not arrived, I am still under spiritual formation and construction, and I am certainly still getting to know the Lord. However, much of the spiritual growth and maturity that has taken place in my life and, in large part, the degree to which I have come to know the Lord, can be attributed to the early years of my walk with Him when the Lord brought a spiritual father into my life. It is not my intention to make this a spiritual autobiography. It is merely to highlight the fact that in my experience, the person who was ordained to lead me to accept Jesus as my Lord and Savior, was not the spiritual father ordained to provide the example and impartation that I needed during those formative years of my spiritual walk with the Lord. Though my reference has been to the earlier stages of my spiritual journey, since divine destiny will often include a person going through numerous phases and stages of spiritual growth and development, the fact remains that the Lord could send a spiritual father into a person's life without regard to the length of time they've been walking with Him or where they may be in their spiritual

> The person whom God uses to bring an individual to acknowledging Jesus as Lord and Savior will very often be a different person than the spiritual father who is ordained to provide the spiritual example and impartation regarding the spiritual formation associated with that individual's God-ordained destiny.

journey. However, for the sake of not setting oneself up for undue disappointment, it is important to remember the apostle Paul's admonition to the Corinthians: *"For though you have ten thousand instructors in Christ, yet have ye not many fathers."* Again, it bears repeating that a God-ordained relationship with a spiritual father is of great benefit. In my opinion, there is no substitute for its spiritual value. As it relates to the proper discernment of an ordained relationship with a spiritual father, however, it is important to understand, even though an individual may be a wealth of knowledge, well-informed, and committed to seeing you succeed, it does not necessarily mean that person is ordained to serve as your spiritual father. Hence, for those people who recognize that a relationship with a spiritual father is among those relationships associated with destiny, it is important to understand that, all things considered, true spiritual fathers are "few and far between." Great care, therefore, should be taken and much consideration given regarding proper discernment in identifying them. A very helpful part of this process is to understand that instructors/mentors and spiritual fathers are not one and the same!

SECTION 4 STUDY QUESTIONS

1. Have you ever had a spiritual father? Who is/ was this? What is/was their most significant contribution to your life?

2. Has reading this section impacted your view of the role a spiritual father regarding spiritual formation? If so, how?

3. Do you feel that your destiny will require significant spiritual formation? Why or Why not?

4. At this stage in your life, how beneficial is/ would be a relationship with a spiritual father? Why?

THE NEED FOR POSITIONING

As mentioned previously, divine destiny will require not only the cultivation of our personal relationship with God, but will also require the proper cultivation of relationships with other people. This was certainly true for Jesus during His life and ministry on the earth, and it is clearly communicated in Scripture.

"And Jesus increased in wisdom and stature, and in favour with God and man." (Luke 2:52)

Given that everything the Word of God communicates about the life and earthly ministry of Jesus has to do with His destiny as it relates to His purpose for coming to Earth, the above Scripture states, very profoundly, that God's plan for Jesus' life necessitated Jesus having favor with both God and with man. In other words, in order for Jesus to fulfill His destiny and purpose for coming into this world, He had to be intentional about developing His ordained relationship with God while also discerning people and developing God-ordained relationships with them. So, if this rings true for Jesus during His time on Earth, it is certainly erroneous and, perhaps, arrogant for anyone else to think that the destiny

God has established for that person's life does not include relationships with both "God and man." Jesus' keenness in properly discerning people and their roles was a significant part of the overall
scope of His destiny and purpose, and it was evident immediately
as He began His earthly ministry.

> *"Then cometh Jesus from Galilee to Jordan unto John, to
> be baptized of him. But John forbad him, saying, I have
> need to be baptized of thee, and comest thou to me? And
> Jesus answering said unto him, Suffer it to be so now: for
> thus it becometh us to fulfil all righteousness. Then he suf-
> fered him."* (Matthew 3:13–15)

In verse 15, when Jesus said, "Suffer it to be so now: for thus it
becometh us to fulfill all righteousness." in response to John's suggestion that he should be baptized by Jesus, it was a clear illustration of Jesus' astuteness in discerning John the Baptist and his
God-ordained role in Jesus' life and ministry. Jesus recognized
that His destiny, as it related to His purpose for coming into this
world, included Him being baptized by John, not vice versa. Jesus
discerned John the Baptist to be the forerunner who would prepare
the way for Him.

> *"The voice of him that crieth in the wilderness, Prepare ye
> the way of the LORD, make straight in the desert a high-
> way for our God."* (Isaiah 40:3)

Contained in this verse of Scripture is one of the most profound
lessons that a person can learn about God-ordained destiny. It
plainly communicates that a time would come when a man would
prepare the way for God. Truthfully, though Jesus was and remains God, His purpose for coming into this world as a man could
only be fulfilled by John preparing the way for Him. As such, everyone should understand that while it is God who establishes and
ordains a person's destiny, He will use people to prepare the ways
into which destiny is to be entered. Jesus understood that as a part
of the process associated with His destiny and purpose, He needed
to be baptized by John. However, Jesus also understood that bap-

tizing Him was not the only role that John the Baptist was to play in preparing the way for Him. In addition to baptizing Jesus, John the Baptist introduced Jesus to the nation of Israel.

> *"John answered them, saying, I baptize with water: but there standeth one among you, whom ye know not; He it is, who coming after me is preferred before me, whose shoe's latchet I am not worthy to unloose."* (John 1:26–27)

> *"The next day John seeth Jesus coming unto him, and saith, Behold the Lamb of God, which taketh away the sin of the world. This is he of whom I said, After me cometh a man which is preferred before me: for he was before me. And I knew him not: but that he should be made manifest to Israel, therefore am I come baptizing with water."* (John 1:29–31)

These Scriptures serve to give anyone committed to the fulfillment of their God-ordained destiny pause to carefully consider the fact that so much of what God has ordained for a person's life will only be accessed by way of a God-ordained introduction. Until John the Baptist introduced Jesus, though He was God manifested in flesh, Jesus was unknown to the nation of Israel. The people who were a part of the masses and who came to hear and be baptized by John had no idea that Jesus—their promised Messiah—was among them. However, all of that changed when John identified Jesus and announced He was the Lamb of God. Though Jesus was the Son of God in the earth and destined to be the Savior of the world, prior to John's introduction, Jesus did not have the level of recognition needed for Him to fulfill the assignment associated with His purpose for coming into this

> Everyone should understand that while it is God who establishes and ordains a person's destiny, He will use people to prepare the ways into which destiny is to be entered.

world. In keeping with his role in Jesus' life, when John introduced Jesus as the "Lamb of God" and announced that Jesus was the person about whom he had been speaking and preaching, Jesus obtained the level of recognition He needed at that time in His life and ministry. Jesus' destiny and purpose for coming into this world as ordained and established by God was such that John the Baptist's introduction of Him to Israel was needful because it moved Jesus from the background to the forefront—a cornerstone of their relationship, and its relative importance should not be minimized. Some hold it was the Father's declaration that Jesus was His Son at the time John baptized Jesus that served to identify and introduce Jesus to Israel. This is an assertion not supported by the Word of God.

> *"And Jesus, when he was baptized, went up straightway out of the water: and, lo, the heavens were opened unto him, and he saw the Spirit of God descending like a dove, and lighting upon him: And lo a voice from heaven, saying, This is my beloved Son, in whom I am well pleased."* (Matthew 3:16–17)

> *"And straightway coming up out of the water, he saw the heavens opened, and the Spirit like a dove descending upon him: And there came a voice from heaven, saying, Thou art my beloved Son, in whom I am well pleased."* (Mark 1:10–11)

> *"And John bare record, saying, I saw the Spirit descending from heaven like a dove, and it abode upon him. And I knew him not: but he that sent me to baptize with water, the same said unto me, Upon whom thou shalt see the Spirit descending, and remaining on him, the same is he which baptizeth with the Holy Ghost. And I saw, and bare record that this is the Son of God."* (John 1:32–34)

Nowhere in the Scriptures above does the Bible indicate the Father's declaration from Heaven that Jesus was His *Beloved* Son identify or introduce Jesus to the masses that came to hear and be baptized by John. In fact, a careful analogy of these Scriptures indicates that all of the activity contained in them—the heavens opening, the Spirit of God appearing as a dove and descending upon Jesus, and the Father's declaration that Jesus was His *Beloved* Son—was seen and heard only by Jesus and John. Nothing in the Scriptures referenced served to communicate to the masses that Jesus was, in fact, the Savior whom Israel had been expecting. The revelation they were expecting came by way of John the Baptist's introduction of Jesus in John 1:29.

Not only did John's announcement serve as an introduction, it also served as affirmation and validation. Previously, I mentioned that John's introduction was needful regarding the positioning of Jesus to fulfill His destiny. In addition to introducing Jesus, John's assertion that Jesus was the Lamb of God also served to publicly affirm and validate Jesus and His ministry—an affirmation and validation that Jesus needed to fulfill His destiny and purpose. Yes, according to the order of God, Jesus, being the Son of God, *needed* John the Baptist's public affirmation to fulfill His ordained destiny and purpose in the earth. John recognized and openly acknowledged that Jesus was greater than he. Although this acknowledgment was true, John's public affirmation and validation were needful to preparing the way for Jesus. That this was true for Jesus should be a wake up call and cause for reconsideration to anyone who believes they can fulfill their destiny by themselves.

> "Divine order" mandates that much of what is needed to fulfill one's destiny will only be accessed when the Lord uses other people to "prepare the way" by affirming and validating that particular person and what he or she is destined to do.

While some may find this hard to accept—regardless of how great a person is destined to be—it is of utmost importance to understand that when it comes to the fulfillment of the destiny that the Lord ordains for a person's life on Earth, "divine order" mandates that much of what is needed to fulfill that destiny will only be accessed when the Lord uses other people to "prepare the way" by affirming and validating that particular person and what he or she is destined to do. Jesus *needed* the recognition that He gained from John the Baptist's introduction. By far, in addition to recognition, John's introduction also provided Jesus with something else that He needed at the time: credibility.

When John announced Jesus as the Lamb of God and as the person about whom John had been speaking and preaching, it was affirmation that served as an endorsement of Jesus, which made Him credible in the eyes of the people who had, for some time, gathered to hear John. This was *credibility* Jesus needed. When Jesus went to John, Jesus was, without question, the best person on planet Earth—He was holy, righteous, and sinless. However, with all His attributes, what John said about Jesus gave Him more credibility in the eyes of the people in Israel who were expecting Him than the fact that He was God manifested in the flesh. According to the divine order and plan of God, John the Baptist's introduction and endorsement of Jesus were essential in preparing the way for Him to fulfill His assignment. Without question, the fulfillment of Jesus' destiny and His purpose for coming into this world was linked to John and should serve to dispel any notion of anyone being "good enough" to fulfill their God-ordained destiny alone. As a matter of fact, it was John's initial introduction and endorsement of Jesus that caused many people to lend their attention to Jesus, as well as to consider Him worthy of being heard. This is quite noteworthy, regardless of what a person's destiny may entail. It can also be particularly helpful to people who understand that the fulfillment of their destiny will require the effective communication of what

> According to the divine order and plan of God, John the Baptist's introduction and endorsement of Jesus were essential in preparing the way for Jesus to fulfill His assignment.

the Lord has established for them to do and ordained them to say. It highlights a dynamic I believe warrants consideration that can be very helpful in this regard, which is, to a great extent, whoever introduces you will determine how you are viewed and heard.

Though Jesus was more gifted and certainly did greater things than John, it was John's gifting that prepared the way for Jesus. This is a reality I have often referenced when speaking with younger and gifted ministers who are obviously destined to do great things. I have said to more of them than I can remember, "God can use the right person's endorsement to do more in one conversation, to position you to fulfill your ordained destiny, than the best 100 sermons you have ever preached." While I am aware everyone who reads this book will not be a minister, I believe that understanding this dynamic can be helpful, regardless of a person's destiny and purpose in life.

> I believe people who have recognized they are destined to do great things for the Lord should understand and respect: submission.

Understanding John's role in preparing the way for Jesus has given me a greater appreciation of another issue that I believe people who have recognized they are destined to do great things for the Lord should understand and respect: submission. As stated previously, Jesus' response to John's suggestion that John should be baptized by Jesus was a very clear display of Jesus' awareness of the role in which John was ordained to play in Jesus' life and ministry. In addition, it was also a profound display of Jesus submitting Himself to the spiritual authority of John the Baptist, the person ordained of God to baptize Him. While this may seem to have been of little consequence as it related to Jesus' destiny and purpose, its significance is seen when considering it was not until after Jesus submitted Himself to the spiritual authority given to John the Baptist that the heavens were opened and the Spirit of God came upon Jesus and empowered Him with the spiritual authority to fulfill His destiny and purpose in the earth.

> *"And it came to pass in those days, that Jesus came from Nazareth of Galilee, and was baptized of John in Jordan. And straightway coming up out of the water, he saw the heavens opened, and the Spirit like a dove descending upon him: And there came a voice from heaven, saying, Thou art my beloved Son, in whom I am well pleased."* (Mark 1:9–11)

While there are those who suggest that Jesus worked miracles and was perhaps involved in other ministry-related activity—associated with His destiny and purpose—*before* He was baptized, this is not supported in Scripture. The truth is that *Jesus did not receive the spiritual authority He needed to fulfill His earthly assignment until after He was baptized by John.* I believe this is because, from the Father's perspective, John's baptism served as Jesus' ministerial inauguration. This was an inauguration that positioned Him to receive the spiritual authority He needed to accomplish the things associated with His earthly ministry and assignment; submission to John's spiritual authority was a part of positioning Jesus to receive the spiritual authority necessary for Him to do these things. This should serve to clarify to anyone—who recognizes that their destiny will require spiritual authority coming from God—that a major part of ensuring God releases that authority to them is their willingness to submit themselves to the spiritual authority of those ordained of God to "prepare the way" for them. As this was notably acceptable to Jesus, it should be acceptable to those who "follow Him" and His example.

SECTION 5 STUDY QUESTIONS

1. How has this section impacted your view of submission to spiritual authority?

2. How vital do think submission to spiritual authority is to your destiny?

3. Do you think the fulfillment of your God-ordained destiny will require someone else's endorsement/validation? Why or why not?

4. Can you identify those who are, or could potentially be, ordained of God to "prepare the way" for you to fulfill your God-ordained destiny? If so, who are they? If not, how committed are you to identifying them?

THOSE CLOSE AND CLOSER

With John's endorsement and baptism, and the Spirit coming upon Jesus, the "way" was fully prepared. Jesus was *perfectly positioned* and *fully empowered* to fulfill the destiny and purpose for which He came into the world. After returning from the wilderness, he proceeded to carry out the mandates of His assignment as the Redeemer of fallen humanity. Given all the dynamics commonly associated with the ministry of Jesus—preaching, healing, miracles, authority, power, and so much more—it is easy to overlook the vital role that keen discernment of people and their places played in the fulfillment of Jesus' destiny and purpose on Earth. However, Scripture clearly communicates that Jesus understood the gravity of these dynamics.

"And it came to pass in those days, that he went out into a mountain to pray, and continued all night in prayer to God. And when it was day, he called unto him his disciples: and of them he chose twelve, whom also he named apostles;" (Luke 6:12–13)

The aforementioned Scriptures reveal that before choosing His disciples, Jesus prayed all night. This indicates the seriousness with which Jesus engaged His decision. Moreover, it shows how seriously He took the issue of properly discerning people and their ordained place and roles in His life and ministry. Jesus understood that a part of His ability to fulfill His destiny and purpose for coming into the world was for His disciples to be people whom the Father had ordained to be with Him during the time of His earthly ministry. The fact that this necessitated all-night prayer gives a clear indication that determining *who* were the disciples was not something that just came to Jesus through osmosis or just because He was the Son of God. It came by way of Him praying and seeking the Father for the ability to properly discern the individuals who were ordained to be His disciples and the people closest to Him.

> Jesus understood that a part of His ability to fulfill His destiny and purpose for coming into the world was for His disciples to be people whom the Father had ordained to be with Him during the time of His earthly ministry.

The identity of people and their places and roles in Jesus' earthly life and ministry were determined by seeking God in prayer. This speaks volumes to the importance of seeking God in this regard, and to the fact that Jesus' personal feelings seemed to have nothing to do with who was chosen, which is noteworthy in its own right. Jesus' will, in regard to choosing the disciples, as always, was to do the will of the Father (John 4:34, 6:38). As it related to choosing and ordaining the disciples, through seeking God in prayer, the fact is *Jesus chose those who had been chosen for Him, according to the will of the Father.* While Luke 6:12–13 elaborates on Jesus' commitment to the astute and proper discernment of the people who were ordained to be His disciples, the manner in which Jesus interacted with His disciples as individuals and collectively throughout His ministry on Earth provides evidence of Jesus' awareness of the importance of dealing with the disciples in accordance with their ordained place in His life. As mentioned previously, in assessing people and their roles in our lives, it is very helpful to consider the fact that Jesus never sought to treat everyone with whom He had a relationship in the same way. In large part, His treatment of people was based on His discernment of them as it related to *their* place and roles in His life and ministry. While the full depth and scope of the rationale and reasons behind Jesus' treatment of the people whom He encountered during His earthly ministry would be too extensive for this writing, the fact that Jesus primarily dealt with people according to His knowledge and understanding of where they "fit" in terms of their ordained place and purpose in His life and ministry is something that I believe a *common occurrence* between Jesus and His twelve disciples will serve to highlight.

> Jesus' treatment of people was based on His discernment of them as it related to *their* place and roles in His life and ministry.

It is common knowledge among people familiar with the Bible that during His earthly ministry, Jesus would often take Peter, James, and John with Him while leaving His other nine disciples behind (Matthew 17:1; Mark 5:37, 13:3, 14:33; Luke 8:51). This common occurrence was due to Jesus' knowledge that in order for them to fulfill their destiny, Peter, James, and John needed to spend more time with Him and be exposed to more things than the other nine. The Word of God gives no indication that Jesus concerned Himself with how the other disciples felt about the noticeable difference in how He interacted with Peter, James, and John. This is yet another lesson in how people should approach relationships once they have adequately discerned others' ordained places and roles. It is important that an unapologetic approach be taken regarding the care and commitment to such ordained relationships, regardless of the feelings this may create in others.

I believe there was never an occasion when Jesus returned and apologized to the other nine disciples for not involving them in the times and events in which He only took Peter, James, and John. I make this observation because I know of too many instances in which relationships that were God-ordained to bear much fruit and to glorify God in great ways never produced the results God desired because of an unhealthy concern among people involved for the feelings that the relationship produced in others. I am not suggesting that we are ever justified in not giving the proper attention to how our relationships affect others, particularly the people closest to us. My aim is to point out that to be overly concerned with other people's feelings when it comes to God-ordained relationships can be the catalyst that negates the manifestation of God's plans and purposes in relationships that He has ordained to bring Him glory. The barometer for measuring how Jesus interacted with Peter, James, John, the other disciples, and everyone else with whom He encountered was *not* how His interaction with them made others feel. It was determined by what Jesus discerned to be the will of the Father. For many people, I think a better understanding of the manner in which Jesus viewed and approached relationships is something that can be both liberating and challenging. It is liberating, because it frees people committed to seeing their destiny fulfilled to interact with others according to the will of God, which God will always grant the grace to do, without undue regard for the opinions of others. It is challenging because it drives home the fact that proper discernment of people and where they fit in regard to their ordained place and roles in our lives should always be a high priority.

It is important that an unapologetic approach be taken regarding the care and commitment to ordained relationships, regardless of the feelings this may create in others.

Jesus was not cavalier about discerning people and determining their place and roles in His life and ministry, nor did He approach the matter haphazardly or leave it to chance. He understood the significance in making the right choices in His life. Actually, Jesus' choices were not only vital to the three-and-a-half year span of His earthly ministry; these choices were of *eternal* consequence. So, by viewing *every* disciple through the lens of their purpose and role, Jesus recognized that the Father's plan mandated He spend more time with Peter, James, and John. In doing so, Jesus' three-and-a-half year investment yielded a return with eternal benefit. I believe the primary reason Jesus spent more time with Peter, James, and John was because of their ordained roles in the Lord's church.

With the exception of Judas, there is no question in my mind that every one of the apostles had a part and role in the church *after* it was birthed on the day of Pentecost in Acts, Chapter 2. However, the New Testament clearly communicates that Peter, James, and John impacted the Lord's church in its birth and infancy in ways that were unmatched by the other apostles who were among Jesus' original twelve. Scripture conveys this truth in the following books:

> To be overly concerned with other people's feelings when it comes to God-ordained relationships can be the catalyst that negates the manifestation of God's plans and purpose in relationships that He has ordained to bring Him glory.

- Book of Acts 2:14–41; Chapter 3, 4:8–13; Chapter 10, etc.
- Book of James
- 1st and 2nd Peter
- 1st, 2nd and 3rd John; and
- Book of Revelation.

While the apostle Paul received much revelation, which led him to write most of the New Testament, it should not be overlooked that a time came in his ministry when he saw the need to seek out and spend time with Peter.

"Then after three years I went up to Jerusalem to see Peter, and abode with him fifteen days." (Galatians 1:18)

The Word of God does not give specifics about the things that Peter discussed with Paul, but the Scripture above records that they spent 15 days together. This indicates the extensive and substantive nature of the things Peter shared with Paul—things that probably made Paul more effective as an apostle to the gentiles and most likely included some things that Peter learned in those times when Jesus took Peter, James, and John with Him and left the other nine disciples behind. *Not* because Peter, James and John were more valuable to God than the others, but because it was needful in order for them to fulfill the destiny and purpose that God ordained for their lives. The way that Jesus chose and dealt with His disciples helps to paint a clear picture of how Jesus interacted with the people closest to Him during His time on Earth. However, in carefully considering the biblical account of how Jesus interacted with everyone whom He encountered, it becomes clear that Jesus made his determination and acted according to the directive of the divine plan and purpose the Father had determined for His life. ***May this be the goal of everyone who reads this book!***

SECTION 6 STUDY QUESTIONS

1. Did you try to treat everyone the same way before reading this section? Why or why not?

2. Has reading this section influenced your view concerning how much time you spend with others? If so, How?

3. Does the fact that Jesus spent more time with Peter, James and John than with the other disciples affect your view of how much time you should spend with people? If, so, how?

SUMMARY

In my previous book, *A Return to Sonship: Understanding Your Spiritual DNA*, I highlighted the spiritual legality that made it necessary for Jesus to reside on Earth as a man as a part of redeeming fallen humanity. Though this is not the focus of this current book, it is a tool that can serve to teach one of the most profound lessons associated with the principle of God's use of people in positioning us to fulfill our God-ordained destiny and purpose in the earth.

The twelve whom Jesus chose to be with Him during His earthly ministry learned the things they needed to learn from Jesus Himself. This was possible because, at the time, Jesus was residing on Earth as a man, which is what made His personal and direct interaction with His disciples spiritually legal, according to God's divine order. However, once He returned to heaven, it was no longer spiritually legal for him to prepare others for the destiny that God ordains for them without including people who reside in the earth in the process. This is a spiritual law that, though often

> The twelve whom Jesus chose to be with Him during His earthly ministry learned the things they needed to learn from Jesus Himself. However, once He returned to heaven, it was no longer spiritually legal for him to prepare others for the destiny that God ordains for them without including people who reside in the earth in the process.

overlooked, is very much a part of Jesus' response and instruction to Saul during his initial encounter with the Lord on the Damascus Road.

> *"And as he journeyed, he came near Damascus: and suddenly there shined round about him a light from heaven: And he fell to the earth, and heard a voice saying unto him, Saul, Saul, why persecutest thou me? And he said, Who art thou, LORD? And the LORD said, I am Jesus whom thou persecutest: it is hard for thee to kick against the pricks. And he trembling and astonished said, LORD, what wilt thou have me to do? And the LORD said unto him, Arise, and go into the city, and it shall be told thee what thou must do."* (Acts 9:3–6)

And he said, Who art thou, LORD? And the LORD said, I am Jesus whom thou persecutest: it is hard for thee to kick against the pricks.

> *"Then Ananias answered, LORD, I have heard by many of this man, how much evil he hath done to thy saints at Jerusalem: And here he hath authority from the chief priests to bind all that call on thy name. But the LORD said unto him, Go thy way: for he is a chosen vessel unto me, to bear my name before the Gentiles, and kings, and the children of Israel: For I will shew him how great things he must suffer for my name's sake. And Ananias went his way, and entered into the house; and putting his hands on him said, Brother Saul, the LORD, even Jesus, that appeared unto thee in the way as thou camest, hath sent me, that thou mightest receive thy sight, and be filled with the Holy Ghost."* (Acts 9:13–17)

These Scriptures contain Saul's inquiry in reference to the Lord's identity and what He would have Saul to do (Acts 9:5–6). As such, they have received much attention. What is often overlooked is the fact that, although Jesus did divulge His identity, He did not communicate to Saul anything relating to his ordained destiny and purpose. Instead, Jesus responded in a way that was a profound exhibition of His adherence to spiritual law and principle associated with the divine pattern of positioning people to fulfill their God-ordained destiny and purpose in this world. The Lord instructed Saul to go to a place where he would be told what the Lord would have him to do. Then, the Lord articulated to Ananias the things Saul had been chosen to do and the role that Ananias would play in facilitating the Lord's will and purpose for Saul's life by positioning him to receive the Holy Ghost. In this regard, just as John prepared the way for Jesus, Ananias prepared the way for Saul. In doing so, he positioned Saul to go on to become known as the apostle Paul and to do great things for the Lord. In light of the events that allowed Saul to become Paul and Ananias to play a role in the Lord's destiny for Paul's life, we yet again have biblical proof that it is of the utmost importance that people who are wholly given to the fulfillment of their destiny embrace the fact that—in some way, shape or form—this will involve the Lord using other people to "prepare the way" that positions them to be empowered by God to fulfill the destiny and purpose that He has ordained and established for their lives.

> God's plan for fulfilling the destiny that He ordains and establishes for every person on Earth has always included and involved—and will always include and involve—other people.

When it comes to the destiny that God establishes for anyone, "people matter." God's plan for fulfilling the destiny that He ordains and establishes for every person on Earth has always included and involved—and will always include and involve—other people. To dismiss or ignore this truth is to reject a spiritual law and divine principle that God established for humanity. My sincere hope and desire is that this book serves to bring awareness to the issue of divinely orchestrated relationships and their value.

My prayer is that this book causes you to give careful and constant attention to properly discerning people and their ordained place and roles in your life. Doing this, I am confident, will prove to be a great benefit and a significant key to accessing your God-ordained destiny.

SUMMARY STUDY QUESTIONS

1. After reading this book, will you try to treat everyone the same way? Why or why not?

2. On a scale of 1 - 10, how has reading this book influenced how vital you think relationships with others are to the fulfilment of your God-given destiny?

3. How has reading this book shaped/reshaped your view and approach to relationships?